SPORTS SCIENCE AND TECHNOLOGY IN THE REAL WORLD

by Janet Slingerland

Content Consultant
Daniela Terson de Paleville, PhD
Department of Health & Sport Sciences
University of Louisville

Core Library

An Imprint of Abdo Publishing
abdopublishing.com

abdopublishing.com

Published by Abdo Publishing, a division of ABDO, PO Box 398166, Minneapolis, Minnesota 55439. Copyright © 2017 by Abdo Consulting Group, Inc. International copyrights reserved in all countries. No part of this book may be reproduced in any form without written permission from the publisher. Core Library™ is a trademark and logo of Abdo Publishing.

Printed in the United States of America, North Mankato, Minnesota
082016
012017

Cover Photo: Gustoimages/Science Source
Interior Photos: Gustoimages/Science Source, 1; Justin Sullivan/Sega Sports/Getty Images, 4, 43; Red Line Editorial, 7, 17; Al Goldis/AP Images, 9; Universal History Archive/Getty Images, 12; Science Source, 15; NASA, 20; Keith Srakocic/AP Images, 22; Troy Maben/Boise State University/AP Images, 26; Lenny Ignelzi/AP Images, 29; Anna Omelchenko/Shutterstock Images, 31, 45; Jay LaPrete/AP Images, 33; Joel Page/AP Images, 34; Rick Osentoski/AP Images, 36; Maridav/Shutterstock Images, 40

Editor: Arnold Ringstad
Series Designer: Ryan Gale

Publisher's Cataloging-in-Publication Data

Names: Slingerland, Janet, author.
Title: Sports science and technology in the real world / by Janet Slingerland.
Description: Minneapolis, MN : Abdo Publishing, 2017. | Series: STEM in the real
    world | Includes bibliographical references and index.
Identifiers: LCCN 2016945470 | ISBN 9781680784831 (lib. bdg.) |
    ISBN 9781680798685 (ebook)
Subjects: LCSH: Sports science--Juvenile literature.
Classification: DDC 796--dc23
LC record available at http://lccn.loc.gov/2016945470

CONTENTS

CHAPTER ONE

WHAT IS SPORTS SCIENCE?

A scientist attaches a series of gray, marble-sized spheres to a pitcher's body. The pitcher picks up a baseball and enters a laboratory. Cameras and computers surround him. He stands on a square of green turf. Across the room is a broad net. The pitcher enters his stance. He goes into his throwing motion. He hurls the ball at top speed into the net.

Motion capture technology can help baseball players and other athletes study their performance.

As he moves, dots on a computer screen light up. The cameras track the gray spheres. They send this data to the computer. The computer program draws the scene in 3D. It connects the dots to form a skeleton. Every tiny movement is tracked.

After a few pitches, the athlete and a scientist study the data. They look for areas for improvement. They find the most efficient pitching motion. Together, they have turned raw data into a useful tool. Their work is an example of sports science and technology in action.

Smart Egg

Sports scientists use a wide variety of technologies to help them do their jobs. One high-tech tool is called a BOD POD. It looks like a giant egg. A person sits inside the pod. The BOD POD measures changes in air volume and pressure. It uses this information to estimate body volume and body weight. These numbers show how dense a person's body is. Muscle is more dense than fat. The BOD POD can estimate what percentage of a person's body is made up of fat. Knowing this can help athletes track how well they are meeting their fitness goals.

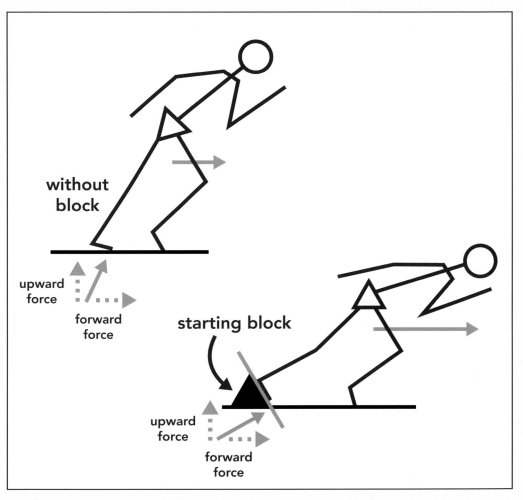

The Biomechanics of a Starting Block

Biomechanists study the forces acting on an athlete. They find ways athletes can use these forces to improve their performance. This illustration shows a runner starting with and without the use of a starting block. Which runner will be able to get a quicker start?

The scientist is a biomechanist. Biomechanists study the forces that act on an athlete's body. They study how muscles and bones move. Different sports involve different movements. A soccer player runs and kicks. A baseball pitcher throws. A football quarterback may run and throw at the same time. A biomechanist can help guide an athlete's training. This can help athletes prevent new injuries.

Some biomechanists work for sporting goods manufacturers. They design clothing and equipment. Others work as consultants for teams. They help athletes identify strengths and weaknesses. They help correct

A biomechanics student tests a new shoe on a plate that measures force.

problems. The ultimate goal is to use science to help athletes win.

Many Sciences, One Purpose

Biomechanics is just one of the many branches of sports science and technology. Each branch focuses on a different area. Anatomy is the study of the body's structures. Physiology is the study of how these structures function. Exercise physiology looks at how exercise affects cells and organs. Nutrition focuses on the food athletes eat. Sports psychology involves training the mind for sports performance. Sports statistics is the study of data, such as batting averages or pitching speed.

No matter what their field of study, sports scientists share common goals. They work to reduce injuries and help athletes be the best they can be.

Dr. Fergus Connolly became the director of performance for the NFL's San Francisco 49ers in 2014. He was interviewed about the use of sports science:

> I believe there are 2 broad areas sports science will impact, injury prevention (or reduction) and improved . . . performance. US sport has clearly pioneered recruitment. . . . However, how you support the recruited athlete is equally important and has huge room for improvement in the US. . . . There's no point in having an elite athlete and not having the systems, resources and environment to support them. It's akin to buying a million dollar sports car and not having the money for engine oil or a service. Sure, it'll manage at first, but eventually fail and perform poorly given time. . . .

> Source: Fergus Connolly. "The Future of Sports Science in America." Interview by Art Horne. Boston Sports Medicine and Performance Group, LLC Blog. BSMPG, June 19, 2013. Web. Accessed April 11, 2016.

Consider Your Audience

Review this passage. Consider how you would adapt it for a different audience, such as your parents or younger friends. Write a blog post conveying the same information for the new audience. How does your approach differ from the original text, and why?

THE HISTORY OF SPORTS SCIENCE

Sports science has been making lots of headlines in recent years. But it is not a new field. Its roots date back thousands of years. It began with basic physiology.

An Ancient Science

In approximately 600 BCE, an Indian doctor named Sushruta prescribed exercise to his patients. He was

People have been training their bodies and competing in physical contests for thousands of years.

the first to do so. He also realized the type of exercise should depend on age, strength, and diet.

The ancient Roman doctors Herodicus and Hippocrates also saw the benefit of exercise. They agreed that diet and exercise worked together to keep a person healthy.

Around 200 CE, Greco-Roman doctor Galen started out as doctor to the gladiators. These warriors were often slaves. They fought each other in large arenas for entertainment. Galen developed training programs and emphasized fitness. He greatly reduced deaths among the fighters.

Galen also investigated the anatomy of both humans and animals. He documented his findings in 16 books. While his books were not totally accurate, doctors relied on them for more than 1,000 years.

The Birth of Nutrition Science

In 1893, 16 chemists put on a demonstration at the Chicago World's Fair. This fair drew people from around the world to learn about culture and the

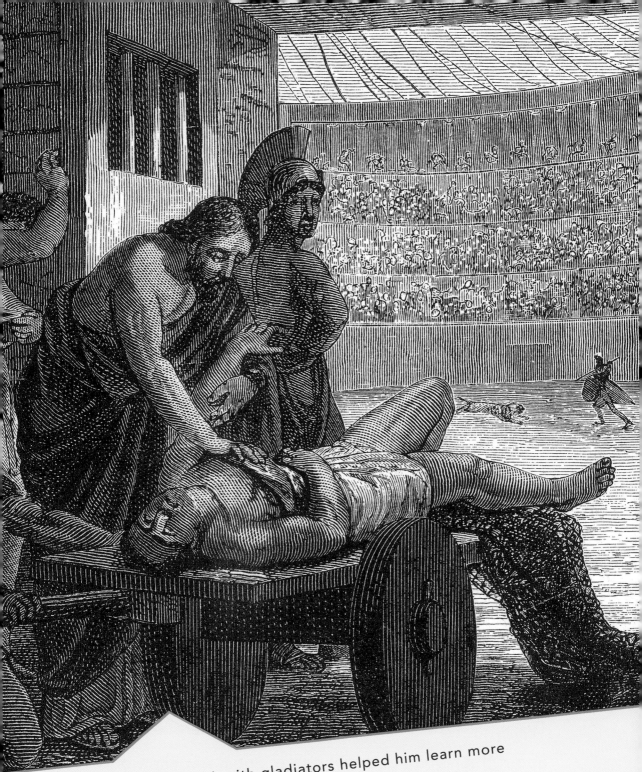

Galen's work with gladiators helped him learn more about fitness.

latest science. The chemists were preparing food and analyzing its nutrients. Before then, food was just something people ate. They thought little about how it affected the body. The team of chemists had been put together by US scientist Wilbur Olin Atwater. He was on a quest to draw people's attention to the science of nutrition.

Atwater developed a way to define food by a few elements: fats, proteins, and carbohydrates. These elements are still called the Atwater factors.

Atwater did not stop there. He studied how many calories people burned doing different activities. He recognized exercising used more calories than relaxing. This let him determine how many calories a person needed to consume daily. Atwater's work began a movement to improve the nutrition and health of the American people.

Breathe Easy

The early 1900s saw other important discoveries about the human body. Danish scientist August Krogh

Name	Calories per gram	Purpose
Carbohydrates	4	Supply energy to the body
Fats	9	Provide energy, transport vitamins, make up protective fat tissue in the body
Proteins	4	Provide energy, used to build most of the body's structures

Nutrients

This chart shows the three major nutrients described by Atwater, along with the number of calories they provide per gram and descriptions of their purpose in the body. Think about the nutrition labels on the foods you eat. What are some foods that are high in each nutrient? How might each nutrient be important for athletes?

determined how oxygen is absorbed into the body. He won the Nobel Prize in Physiology or Medicine in 1920 for this work.

Krogh studied respiration. He analyzed the air people breathe in. He compared it with the air people breathe out. Krogh also studied circulation. This is the movement of blood throughout the body. He researched how these things change when a person exercises. Krogh built his own equipment so he could conduct these studies.

Bicycle Ergometer

In 1910 August Krogh started studying exercise physiology. One tool he wanted was a bicycle ergometer. This would measure the amount of work a person riding a bicycle was doing. Krogh did not like what was already available. So he designed his own. Krogh's designs were so accurate they were used for almost 100 years. Even today many exercise physiology labs have modified Krogh ergometers.

Science Down Under

Sports science really took hold in the late 1900s. After the 1976 Summer Olympics, many Australians were disappointed. Their country's athletes brought home only five medals. None were gold. It was the first time in 40 years Australia hadn't won a gold medal.

In response, the nation created the Australian Institute of Sport (AIS). Scientists at the AIS study exercise physiology, sports psychology, and all other branches of sports science and technology. AIS scientists worked with athletes on a daily basis. The hard work paid off. At the 1984 Summer Olympics,

Australia won 24 medals. Four of them were gold. Australia remains a competitive nation today. Many top sports scientists come from Australia or were trained there.

Exercise in Space

In space, astronauts feel weightless. They float around inside spacecraft and space stations. Gravity does not pull them to the floor. Weightlessness is fun, but it can also be damaging. Muscles and bones weaken when they are not working against gravity all the time. Researchers at

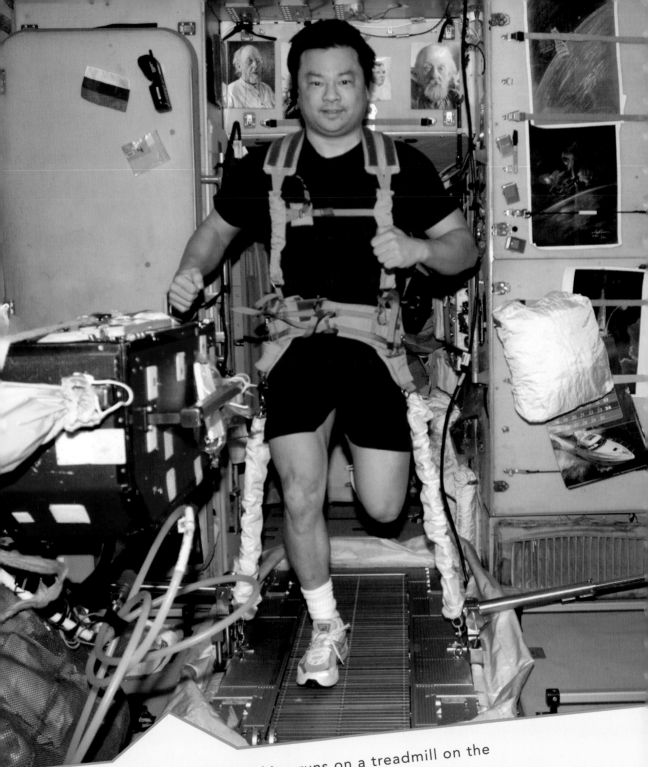

Astronaut Leroy Chiao runs on a treadmill on the
International Space Station.

NASA make sure that astronauts exercise in space to stay healthy.

Astronauts use special treadmills and other exercise machines. These devices have straps to hold the user down so he or she does not float away. Astronauts spend more than two hours each day exercising. Future missions to Mars will require astronauts to live in space for many months. NASA's scientists are learning all they can about exercise in space to make this possible.

EXPLORE ONLINE

Chapter Two highlighted a few key advances in sports science history. The article at the website below offers another brief history of sports science. How is the information in this article similar to what is presented in Chapter Two? What new information did you learn from the website?

Sport Science: A Brief and Interesting History
mycorelibrary.com/sports-science

CAREERS IN SPORTS SCIENCE

Sports scientists work in a variety of settings. Some spend their days in laboratories. Others work on the practice field with sports teams. Some work with the military or entertainers. Others help average people get fit. All deal with sports or fitness.

There are many different careers in sports science. Most require at least a bachelor's degree. Some

Sports science experts may help out on the field as athletes go through drills.

require a graduate degree, such as a master's degree or doctorate. Many types of sports scientists must be certified. This ensures they are experts in their chosen field. This process is set up by an organization connected to the career.

Bodies in Motion

Biomechanists study how the body moves. They usually work in a laboratory. Their work may lead to new clothing and gear. Improved gear can prevent injuries. It allows for free movement. It cools the body where it tends to heat up.

Many biomechanists work for colleges and

universities. Some of these researchers study more than just bodies. They look at the relationship between athletes and playing surfaces. They also look at nonhuman athletes. They study horses and their racetracks. Engineers use this research to develop safer surfaces for humans and animals alike.

Most colleges offer biomechanics as part of a kinesiology program. Some colleges offer degrees in biomechanics. These may be offered as part of a biomedical engineering program. Most careers in biomechanics require a master's degree. Some require a doctorate.

Athletic Trainers

Athletic trainers are sports scientists who

Cars and Turf

The company Viconic Sporting developed padding to go under synthetic turf. The padding looks a bit like a giant egg carton. It helps absorb energy during impact. This puts less force on a player when he or she falls. This padding is not entirely new. A similar material is currently used in many US cars. It helps reduce the impact of car crashes.

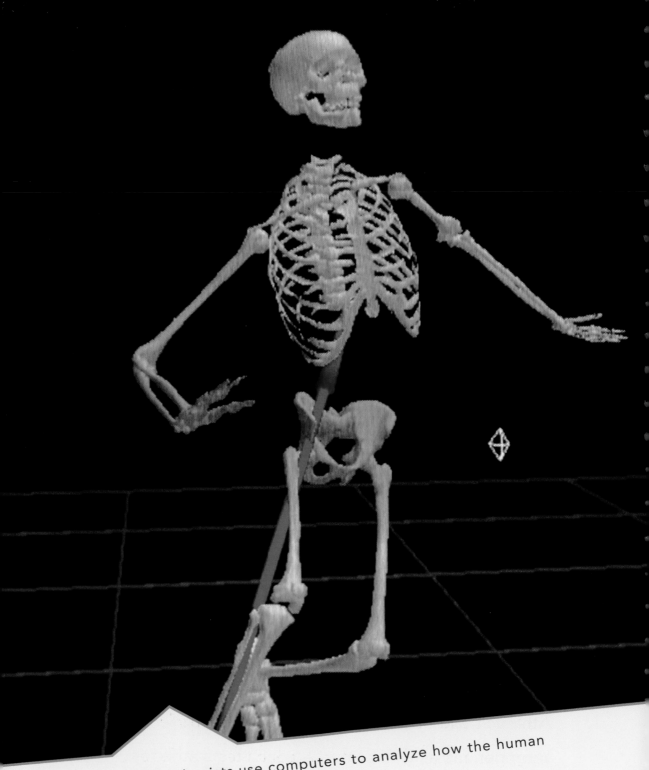

Biomechanists use computers to analyze how the human body moves.

are also health-care professionals. They have four main jobs. They prevent injuries, diagnose medical conditions, take action in emergencies, and help treat and rehabilitate athletes. Before a sporting event, they help athletes warm up and stretch. They may diagnose players with illnesses not related to the sport. During an event, they may treat a small cut, allowing a player to return to the field. Following an event, an athletic trainer may help an athlete cool down and stretch again. After an injury, a trainer may perform physical therapy. He or she helps the athlete return to peak condition.

Athletic trainers must complete a program in athletic training. Most hold at least a master's degree. They must also pass a certification test. To remain certified, they continue to take classes during their career. They keep up with the latest treatments.

Strength and Conditioning Coaches

Strength and conditioning coaches make athletes stronger, faster, and better. A coach tests athletes to see how fit they are. The coach then develops a training program for each person. The goal is to improve the athlete while avoiding injuries.

Most strength and conditioning coaches work as part of a team. The team may be at the professional, college, or even high school level. Strength and conditioning coaches work closely with other coaches.

Some strength and conditioning coaches work in private settings. They may work one-on-one with a few select athletes. They may own a business that trains large numbers of athletes. Strength and conditioning coaches often specialize in a specific sport. Sometimes they train athletes in a variety of sports.

Most strength and conditioning coaches hold a bachelor's or master's degree in a related subject. This could be exercise science, exercise physiology, kinesiology, or another similar program. Some colleges have degrees in strength and conditioning coaching. Once a person obtains a degree, a major

Strength and conditioning coaches often help athletes in the weight room.

strength and conditioning group must certify him or her. One of these groups is the National Strength and Conditioning Association.

Food Is Fuel

Nutritionists understand the chemical makeup of food. They know how the body processes it. Sports nutritionists extend this. They know when athletes need to eat certain foods to improve performance and recovery.

Much of the work sports nutritionists do involves interacting with other people. They work with food services to develop menus for the training table. They make it easier for the athletes to put the right foods on their plates. They educate the athletes on how to eat right when they are on their own.

Many factors can influence athletes' food needs. What sport do they play? Which position do they play? Do they have any allergies? Do they have cultural or religious restrictions? Are they too heavy or too light? Are they traveling? Sports nutritionists

Nutritionists help athletes choose foods that are best for their health.

must know how the answers to all these questions will affect an athlete's ideal diet.

Sports nutritionists are often used as consultants. They usually meet with teams and athletes once or a few times a week. Sometimes they work with athletes on a daily basis. The nutritionists can see how the athletes are performing. Nutrition changes can then be made quickly.

The education for sports nutritionists is challenging. They attend a college program designed for registered dieticians. This involves four years of schooling. The program must be approved by the Academy of Nutrition and Dietetics. Students then complete a nine-month internship. Following graduation, they must pass a test.

Over the next two years, they need to spend at least 1,500 hours working in athletics and wellness. After passing another exam, they become certified in sports dietetics. To maintain this status, they need to

Some universities have special nutrition rooms set aside for student athletes to help the players make healthful choices.

be recertified every five years. This includes working in the field and continuing to take classes.

Mind Games

Many sports scientists help athletes improve their bodies. Sport psychologists help them improve their minds. Athletes seek every advantage they can get. This includes a mental edge.

Sports psychologists cover a wide array of issues. They help athletes maintain focus. They teach athletes

A team sports psychologist, right, speaks with baseball player David Ortiz.

better ways to communicate with their teammates. They help athletes cope with being injured. They work to reduce anxiety.

Some sport psychologists get jobs on a team. Others become consultants. They work with all levels from student to professional. They also deal with nonathletes, such as coaches.

FURTHER EVIDENCE

Chapter Three discusses several careers in the field of sports science and technology. What was one of the main points of this chapter? What evidence was included to support that point? The website below describes some of these careers. Does the information on the website discuss one of the main points of the chapter? Does it present new evidence?

Exercise Science Career Paths
mycorelibrary.com/sports-science

CHAPTER FOUR

THE FUTURE OF SPORTS SCIENCE

Sports science is frequently in the headlines. It does not seem as if this will change anytime soon. Elite athletes will keep looking to science to give them an edge.

One major trend in sports science is individualization. Athletes can use data that is specific to them to help improve performance. Wearable technology can help with this. Coaches can track

Today's top athletes use science to make them the best players possible.

everything an athlete does. This may include sleeping, eating, and training. These items will factor into the athlete's planning.

Using wearable technology, coaches will have access to their players' data during a game. They'll be able to see when a player is reaching his or her maximum effort. They may see when a player is tiring. They can let him or her rest and put in a fresh player.

Wearing Tech

Wearable technology provides much of the data used by sports scientists. One such system is called Catapult. Players wear small devices between their shoulder blades while playing. Scientists monitor data on a nearby computer. Data provided includes speed, height, and direction. Monitors can show player interactions on the playing field. Data can identify players who are becoming tired. Catapult is used in soccer, football, basketball, rowing, and more.

Playing Safer

Sports science is also making great strides in player safety. Wearable technology can show when a player needs rest. Individual training and nutrition programs build stronger athletes. But scientists are also working to better understand injuries.

Efforts to treat concussions in football led to many new innovations. Blood tests may detect signs of a concussion. New padding may reduce the impact of falls. New helmets protect the head and neck better. Many more ideas are still being researched.

Expanding Markets

Sports science is moving into new areas. Experts work with dancers, the military, and entertainers. Sports science can be applied to anything that stresses the human body.

Sports science has already moved to the

IN THE REAL WORLD
Feeding Greatness

Nyree Dardarian is a professor at Drexel University. She is the sports nutritionist for the Philadelphia Union soccer team. Dardarian also helps dancers and entertainers. She makes sure they are properly fueled before a performance. She stresses hydration. Many vocalists do not drink enough liquids. This increases their risk of injury.

Wearable technology, such as fitness watches, can track speed, distance, and heart rate.

general public. People use wearable technology to track the number of steps they walk. Everyday athletes are using gear developed for elite competitors. Sports science and technology benefit everyone, from everyday people to elite athletes. Advances in these fields are making a healthier world.

Dr. F. H. Froes developed new sports materials. An avid golfer, he questioned the ethics of using costly materials in sports:

> *The carbon-fiber vaulting pole, javelins with spiral tails, golf balls with special dimple patterns, stiffer carbon-fiber tennis rackets, bicycles with new types of wheels . . . all lead to "further and faster." Where should this end? Can we ensure that people are competing and not the advanced materials? Certainly, we do not want . . . to go back to a wooden pylon. But how about electronically guided darts, heat-seeking missiles for grouse-shooting . . . solar-energy-enhanced bicycles, and terrain-following golf balls that automatically find the lowest local elevation on a putting surface (the bottom of the hole)?*

Source: F. H. Froes. "Is the Use of Advanced Materials in Sports Equipment Unethical?" JOM 49.2 (1997): 15–19. TMS. The Minerals, Metals, and Materials Society. Web. Accessed April 12, 2016.

Changing Minds

Should athletes be able to use any sports technology? Take a position on this topic. Imagine your friend has an opposing view. Be clear about your opinion and reasons for it. Include details and facts to support your position.

FAST FACTS

- People have been studying the science of sports for thousands of years.
- Discoveries in the late 1800s helped create the modern science of nutrition.
- Sports scientists use a variety of sciences to help athletes be more competitive and less prone to injury.
- Most sports scientists need at least a bachelor's degree for their jobs. Many require a master's degree or additional certification.
- Sports scientists work all over the world. The market for sports scientists is currently growing.
- Sports scientists work with athletes, entertainers, the military, astronauts, and anyone else who needs his or her body to operate as efficiently as possible.
- Athletic trainers are health care providers who specialize in supporting athletes.
- Biomechanics applies the laws of physics and mechanics to human performance.

- Sports nutritionists use their knowledge of nutrition to maximize athletes' performance.
- Sports psychologists apply their knowledge of psychology to help athletes perform better.
- Strength and conditioning coaches use their knowledge of exercise physiology to train athletes.

STOP AND THINK

Tell the Tale

In Chapter One, you read about an athlete undergoing biomechanical testing in a laboratory. Imagine you are an athlete going through this process. Write a story explaining your journey. What do you hope the process will do for you as an athlete? How do you feel as you go through the testing?

Dig Deeper

After reading this book, what questions do you still have about sports science and technology? Is there a specific career that you'd like to know more about? With an adult's help, find a few reliable sources to help you answer your questions. Write a paragraph about what you learned.

Say What?

Studying sports science and technology can mean learning a lot of new vocabulary. Find five words in this book that you have not heard before. Use a dictionary to find out what they mean. Write their meanings in your own words and use each word in a new sentence.

Surprise Me

This book touches on lots of different areas of sports science and technology. After reading the book, what two or three facts did you find most surprising? Write a few sentences about each fact. Include why you found each fact surprising.

GLOSSARY

certification
a process through which people prove they are qualified to practice in a specific field

concussion
a brain injury caused by a bump, blow, or jolt to the head

consultant
a person who is hired to provide expert advice

elite
at the highest level

fitness
the state of being physically healthy and fit

kinesiology
the study of how a body moves

nutrients
elements in food that help a body survive and grow

nutrition
the study of how a body uses food to ensure proper health

performance
how well an athlete plays his or her particular sport

physiology
the branch of biology that looks at the normal functions of a body, including how the body's systems, organs, and cells work

rehabilitate
to restore an athlete to peak performance following illness or injury

LEARN MORE

Books

Labrecque, Ellen. *The Science of a Sprint.* Ann Arbor, MI: Cherry Lake, 2016.

Swanson, Jennifer. *Super Gear: Nanotechnology and Sports Team Up.* Watertown, MA: Charlesbridge, 2016.

Wilsdon, Christina, Patricia Daniels, and Jen Agresta. *Ultimate Body-Pedia.* Washington, DC: National Geographic, 2014.

Websites

To learn more about STEM in the Real World, visit **booklinks.abdopublishing.com**. These links are routinely monitored and updated to provide the most current information available.

Visit **mycorelibrary.com** for free additional tools for teachers and students.

INDEX

ABOUT THE AUTHOR

Janet Slingerland used to play many sports but is now mainly a fan. She especially likes watching ice hockey and motocross. She lives in New Jersey with her husband and three children.